KNOWABOUT

Pattern

KNOWABOUT
Pattern

Text: Henry Pluckrose
Photography: Chris Fairclough

Franklin Watts

London/New York/Sydney/Toronto

© 1988 Franklin Watts
12a Golden Square
London W1

ISBN: 0 86313 654 0
Editor: Ruth Thomson
Design: Edward Kinsey

Typesetting: Keyspools Limited
Printed in Hong Kong

About this book

This book is designed for use in the home, playgroup, and infant school.

Mathematics is part of the child's world. It is not just about interpreting numbers or in mastering the tricks of addition or multiplication. Mathematics is about ideas. These ideas (or concepts) have been developed over the centuries to help explain particular qualities, such as size, weight, height, as well as relationships and comparisons. Yet all too often the important part which an understanding of mathematics will play in a child's development is forgotten or ignored.

Most adults can solve simple mathematical tasks by "doing them in their head". For example, you can probably add up or subtract simple numbers without the need for counters, beads or fingers. Young children find such abstractions almost impossible to master. They need to see, talk, touch and experiment.

The photographs in this book and the text which supports them have been prepared with one major aim. They have been chosen to encourage talk around topics which are essentially mathematical. By talking with you, the young reader will be helped to explore some of the central concepts which underpin mathematics. It is upon an understanding of these concepts that a child's future mastery of mathematics will be built.

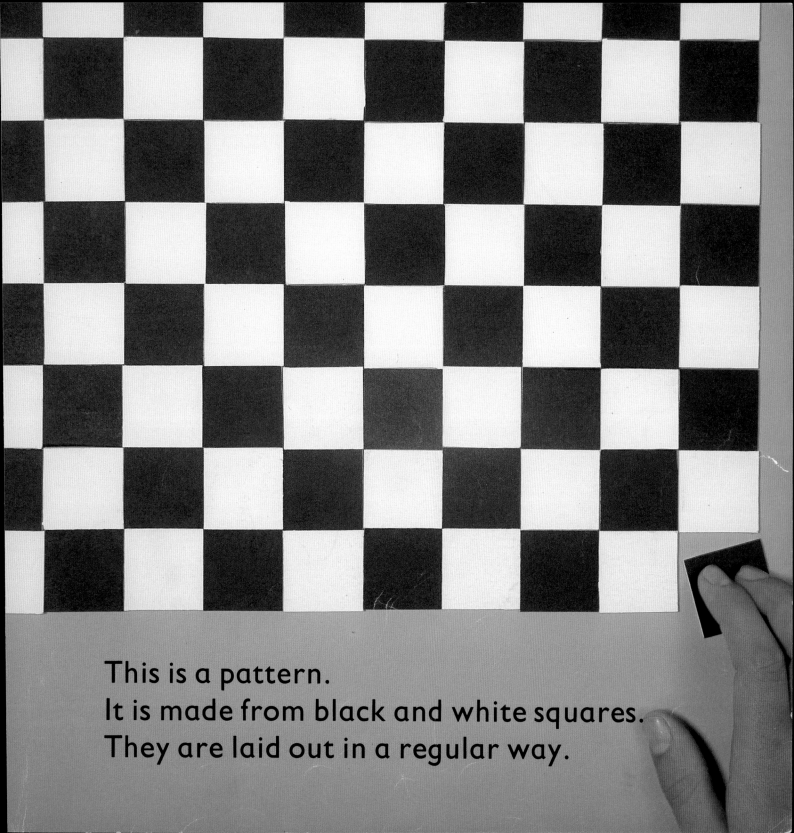

This is a pattern.
It is made from black and white squares.
They are laid out in a regular way.

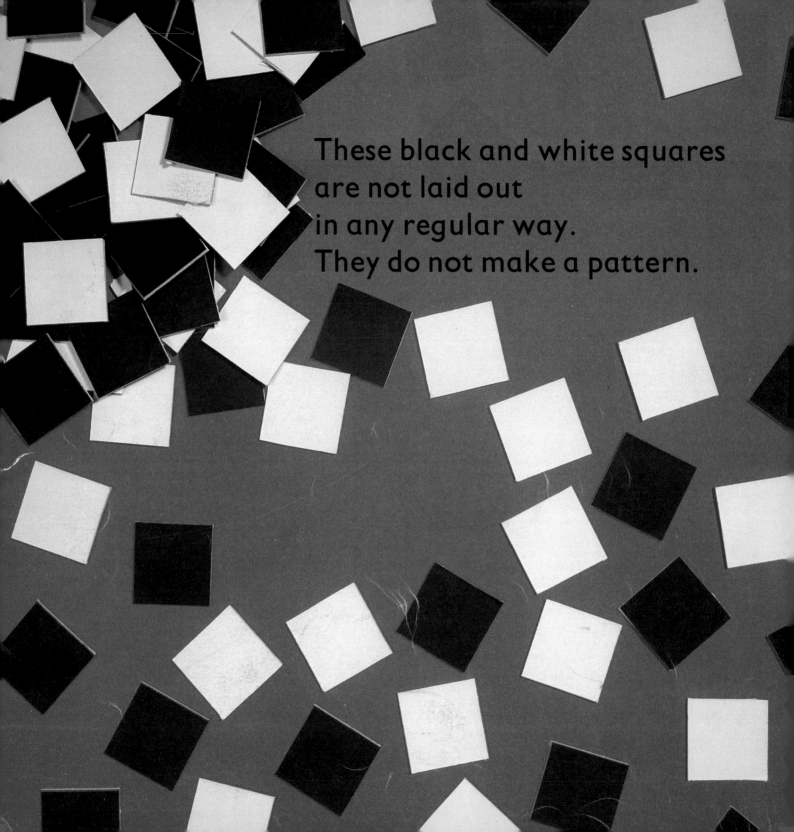

These black and white squares
are not laid out
in any regular way.
They do not make a pattern.

Patterns are all around us.

You can find pattern in nature—
on flower heads . . .

on leaves . . .

and on butterflies.

You can find pattern on carpets . . .

on dishes . . .

and on cloth.

There are patterns
on the soles of shoes.

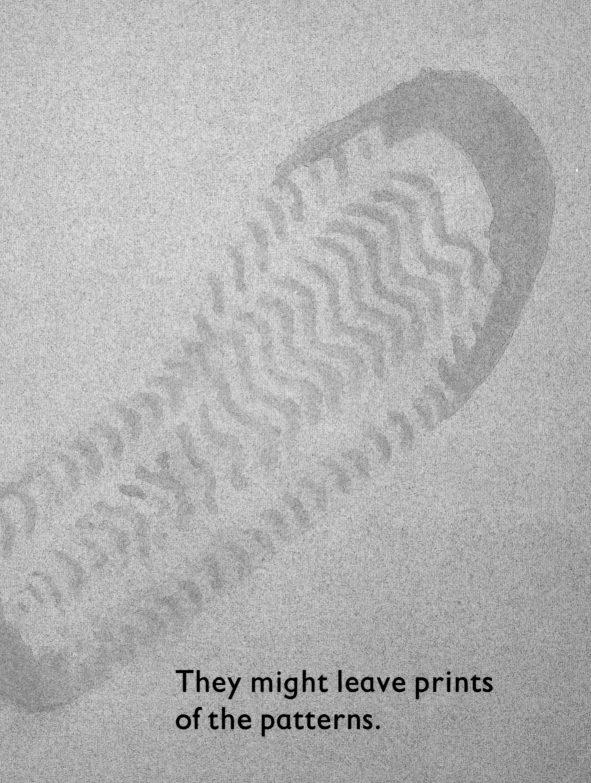

They might leave prints
of the patterns.

Many patterns repeat themselves.
Can you see the repeat in this pattern?

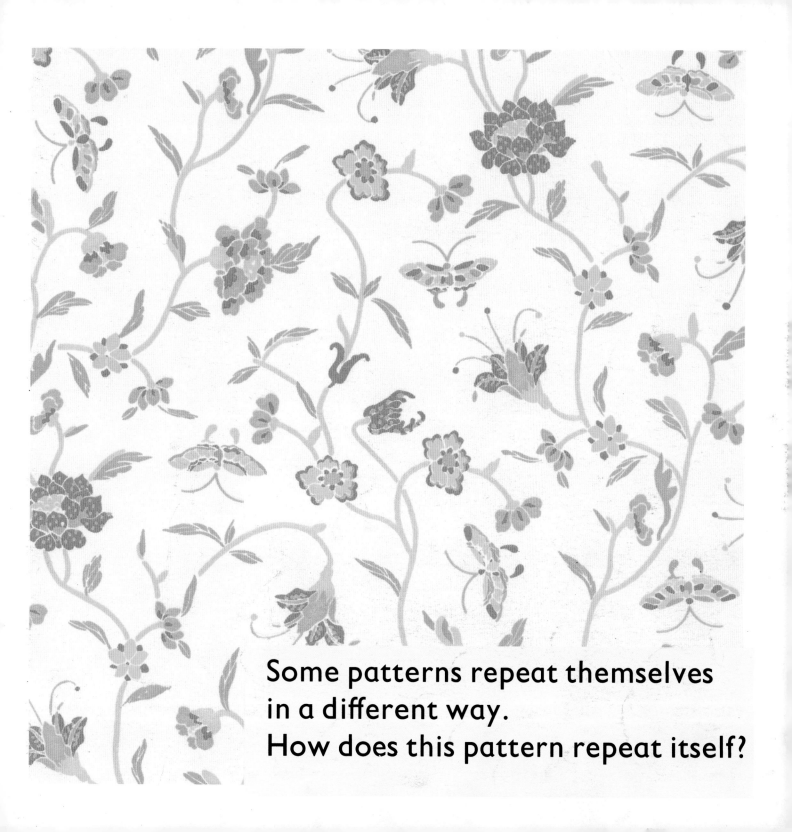

Some patterns repeat themselves
in a different way.
How does this pattern repeat itself?

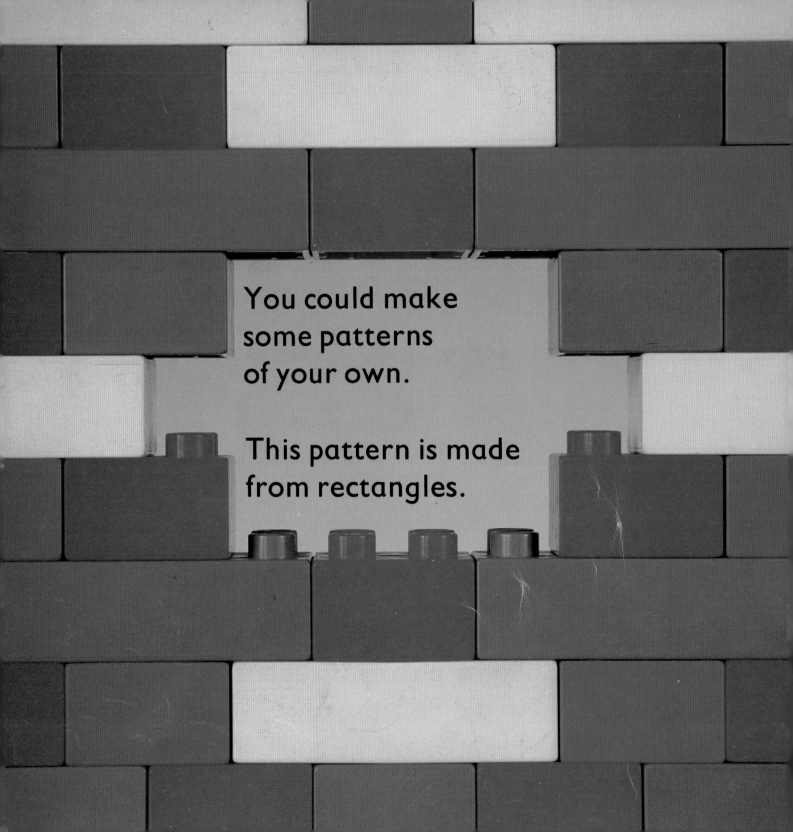

You could make
some patterns
of your own.

This pattern is made
from rectangles.

This one is made from diamonds.

Colour is important in this pattern.

Can you see where the pattern is broken?

Try making some patterns
with leaves . . .

with wooden shapes . . .

with paper . . .

or with paint.

You can make a pattern
by repeating one letter, like this . . .

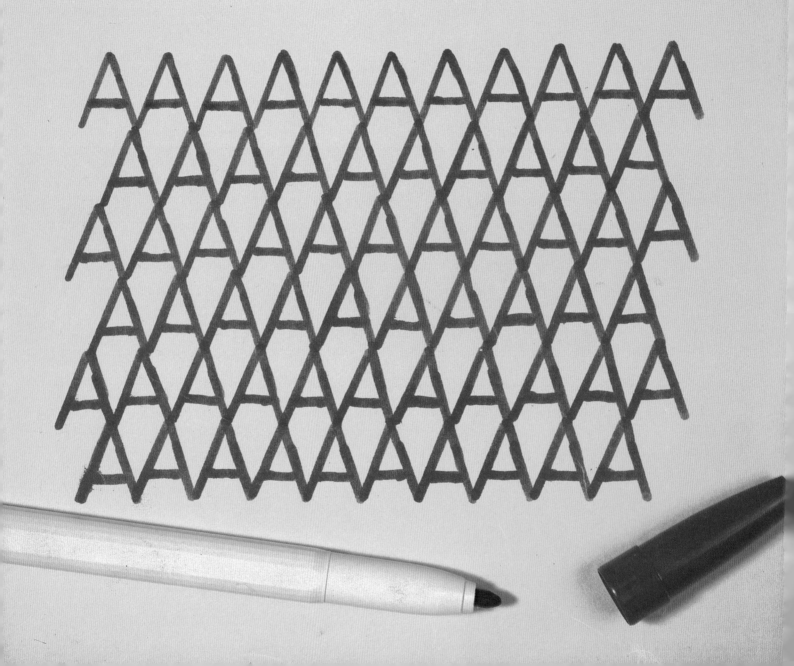

or this.

How many more patterns
can you make?

Look around you.
How many patterns can you see?